Talk-Together

IS ANYONE HOME?

DAVID LE JARS

TWO CAN ™

PRINCETON ■ LONDON

www.two-canpublishing.com

Published in the United States and Canada by
Two-Can Publishing LLC
234 Nassau Street
Princeton, NJ 08542

© 2001 Two-Can Publishing

For information on Two-Can books and multimedia,
call 1-609-921-6700, fax 1-609-921-3349, or visit our Web site at
http://www.two-canpublishing.com

Art Director Ivan Bulloch
Editor Diana James
Assistant Designer Dawn Apperley
Illustrator David Le Jars

'Two-Can' is a trademark of Two-Can Publishing.
Two-Can Publishing is a division of Zenith Entertainment Ltd,
43-45 Dorset Street, London W1U 7NA

hc ISBN 1-58728-014-0
sc ISBN 1-58728-018-3

hc 1 2 3 4 5 6 7 8 9 10 02 01
sc   2 3 4 5 6 7 8 9 10 02

Printed in Hong Kong

Contents

Wake up   4

Let's get dressed   6

In the kitchen   8

Let's play   10

Cleaning up   12

Time to eat!   14

In the garden   16

Living room   18

Party time   20

Bath time   22

Good night   24

Wake up

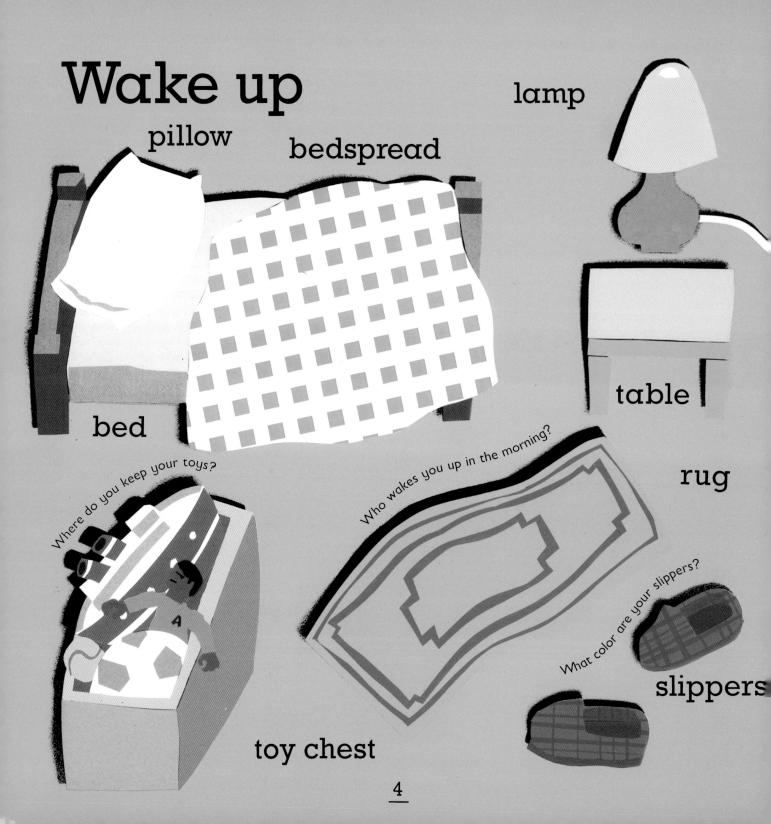

pillow

bedspread

lamp

bed

table

Where do you keep your toys?

Who wakes you up in the morning?

rug

What color are your slippers?

slippers

toy chest

Let's get dressed

blouse

dress

Can you button your blouse?

Where do you keep your clothes?

Can you dress yourself?

skirt

baseball cap

shoes

T-shirt

overalls

shorts

Can you tie your shoelaces?

In the kitchen

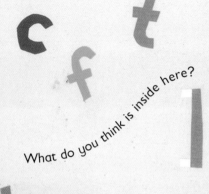

refrigerator

What do you think is inside here?

Where do you put your garbage?

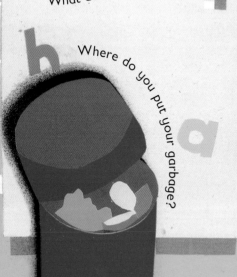

garbage can

What do you have for breakfast?

toaster

tea kettle

sink

Do you wash dishes?

Do you know what this machine does?

washing machine

Who sleeps in this bed?

food
processor

stove

Mmmm - what's cooking?

bowl   mug

9

Let's play

How many rooms are there in the dollhouse?

teddy bear

dollhouse

Can you play a musical instrument?

Do the jigsaw pieces fit in the empty spaces?

paint

jigsaw

drum

What color is the truck?

truck

doll

Why do cars go to a garage?

What can you build with your blocks?

blocks

garage

ball

board game

Cleaning up

iron

Do you help clean the house?

What does this machine do?

ironing board

vacuum cleaner

What happens when you spill a drink on the floor?

mop

bucket

Where do you put your dirty clothes?

dustcloth

dustpan

laundry basket

brush

Is your bedroom always neat?

Time to eat!

bread

What do you use a fork for?

pasta

lettuce

plate

tomato

What do you like to drink?

water

crumbs

spoon

What is your favorite food?

apple

knife

ketchup

French fries

Can you find something very, very cold?

How many green peas can you find?

ice cream

chicken

peas

banana

juice

fork

In the garden

wheeeeeeee!

How high can you jump?

slide

hose

Do you like splashing in water?

wading pool

watering ca

bird feeder

shed

fence

What can you see inside the shed?

What do you use a rake for?

rake

trowel

vegetable garden

spade

flowers

How many flowers can you count?

wheelbarrow

17

Living room

television

Which room do you like best in your home?

pillow

Do you like listening to music?

telephone

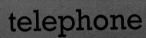

sound system

comic book

painting

Is this a happy picture?

How many books are on this shelf?

shelf

Party time

cookie

card

magician

straw

What's in the hat?

candles

How old are you?

When is your birthday?

juice

present

balloon

cake

What do you like best—cake or a sandwich?

gelatin

Count the candles on the cake.

sandwich

Who has been snacking?

Bath time

sponge

What do you clean your teeth with?

toothpaste

toilet

Can you find a fish in the bathroom?

toy duck

What do you use soap for?

soap

Do you have a favorite bath toy?

shower

bathtub

sink

How many legs does the frog have?

Do you clean your teeth?

toothbrush